I0427132

A Soul at Work

By

Isabel Rojas

authorHOUSE™

1663 LIBERTY DRIVE, SUITE 200
BLOOMINGTON, INDIANA 47403
(800) 839-8640
WWW.AUTHORHOUSE.COM

First published by AuthorHouse 03/07/05

ISBN: 1-4208-2452-X (sc)

Printed in the United States of America
Bloomington, Indiana

This book is printed on acid-free paper.

ACKNOWLEDGEMENTS

I will like to thank god first and foremost, for giving me life and allowing me to grow. Thanks to my friends who have given me unconditional love and support while putting up with me and my indecisiveness. Thanks for putting up with me guys and for being such a great audience, I love you all. Jess & Sovi, thanks for the wonderful advice and for encouraging me in making this book possible. To my sis Evelyn who has always encouraged me and given me a valuable lesson, to believe in myself and to have confidence. (You are the best sis). To my nieces Ashley & Brianna you guys are my world. To my brother Many and Jonathan, I love you guys.

Thank you daddy for your positive presence in the last 31 years of my life I love you. Mom may god bless you and thank you for nourishing me and allowing me to be the women that I am today.

To my little angel in the sky. Finally, to those who understand what is like to express creativity without any concern of criticism go out there and give it all you have, what do you have to loose? make it happen for yourself.

Dedicated to the
Rojas
&
Puentes
Family

TABLE OF CONTENTS

WHAT IS POETRY

What is poetry
One may ask
Poetry can never be define
I must answer
It's a creation of love, experiences
Hidden feelings
Creativity at it's best
A soul that never rest
Working the pages without a break
Digging & digging
Till it strikes gold

Nature at it's best
What is poetry?

Poetry has no definition
And no end
For it flows rhythmically
And it goes express

<u>WILL WE STILL BE FRIENDS</u>

I don't know where to start
I get the feeling we went to far
Can you agree with me

We went beyond our fantasies
Far beyond what we expected
I never thought
I will give you intimacy
But the labor that went into it
Was far more than what I expected

Use this line as a reference
We are friends with outside
Preference
Let's not frown on this experience

I promise you this
We won't ever be exposed but the
Question is
Will we still be friends?

INSPIRATION

Inspiration comes from within
One has to plant that seed
Cultivate it
Only then can one group
Inspiration
Creativity
&
knowledge
to understand
the meaning of inspiration
one has to reach out and
allow to be touched

inspiration

A PICTURE

A picture is worth
Words that cannot
Be express

Moments that cannot
Be relived
Precious memories
Caught in a time capsule
To be viewed forever

<u>LET</u>

Let go and be free

Let love enter within

Let life surprise you

Let pain embrace you
For only then you will learn

Let beauty flourish
Allow sacrifice to enter
For then you will
Learn to appreciate

Let dreams go unfounded
Let inspiration go unblinded

Let go of blame
For only then you will welcome
Acceptance

Let go and be free

<u>LEARNING</u>

Learning to say you are sorry
Frees the mind and soul

Learning to say I love you
Goes a long way
You never know the chance
May never come again

Learning to become independent
Builds confidence and strength

Learning to take responsibility
Makes you a bigger and better person

Learning to have sanity and freedom
Makes you appreciate yourself and the
World around you

Learning is believing
Believing is learning

Learn that learning has no
Limit

A JOYFUL MOMENT IN TIME

A joyful memory
To last an eternity

An unexpected feeling
Transformed into my
Heart

Releasing inside
Slowly making sure
It leaves it's mark

Regenerating around
My soul
Capturing every beat
Of my heart

A joyful moment in time

YOU ARE BLESSED

You know you are blessed
Because god has touched you
And given you life
You are blessed
Because god will never forsake you
The strength you possess
Has been blessed
You are blessed because you
Have open up your heart
Your mouth with prayers
And god has always listen
To you
For he is always available

You are blessed you
Have god by your side

<u>TIME</u>

Time is all we have
Time is all we need

Time is precious
Time is valuable

Take time in all you do

Accomplishments are
made in time

Death takes time
Growing old is all in time
Time has no speed

Time is all we need

<u>SISTER</u>

My sister
You are my friend
You have accepted me
For who I am

You have been there
From the start
Always listening
And giving great advice

I thank you sis
You are one of a kind

Like the sun
You brighten up my life
Your smile
Your wisdom
Your patience
&
your love
never forget
you're #1
in my life
I forever hold you
Dear in my heart

LETTER TO A FRIEND

I wish to remain you
That our friendship
Means the world
To me

You are my sister
My confidant
My mirror
&
my therapist

I thank you
For all those times you
Put up with me and
My nonsense
For the love
&
joy
&
happiness
you have brought into
my life
friend, sister
thank you
I treasure and admire you

Our journey is long but
As long as I have you by
My side I am confident
That everything will be alright

I leave you with these
Lovely words
I am very lucky to have a friend like you

YOU HAVE GROWN

When you love someone else
You have grown
When you learn to accept
Things for what they are
You have grown

When you finally feel complete
You have grown
When you love yourself
You have grown
When you have given more than
What you have received
You have grown

When you learn to have faith
You have grown
When you learn to accept fault
You have grown
When you become non judgmental
You have grown
As you continue to learn
You continue to grow

<u>MY LITTLE GIRLS</u>

My little princess
That's what you both are
A great lovable creation
It brings tears to my eyes
When I think of the
Love & joy
You bring into my life
Two beautiful flowers
Two beautiful roses
Blossoming and growing

My little girls

PRICELESS TREASURE

Love trust
And friendship
That's what I require

A new beginning
A new heart
&
a new love
harmony is waiting
to fulfill my heart

new awakening
new beginning
new life
&
love
that's what I seek
and yearn for

the value of it all
is a priceless treasure

<u>A GLOW</u>

Every time I close my eyes
It's there
Shinning oh so beautifully

It embraces my heart
And gives rhythm to my soul

A permanent smile deep within

It's like magic unfolding

I am forever blessed
With this precious glow

<u>MY LITTLE BROTHER</u>

Joy
Love & happiness
You brought into my life
The day you entered this world

I love you like no other
For your love is unconditional

My world is now complete
You taught me the meaning
Of love
Joy & strength

For you I will move mountains
And swim across the deepest sea

My love for you continues
To grow as you venture the earth
Remember little brother
I am here for you
I am not going anywhere

We will always be together
Side by side

My little brother
My life

<u>CRAVE</u>

I crave your touch
I crave your voice
Your lips
Your body

My desire for you
Goes unnourished

I want to feel your
Hands tracing down
My body

Your warm lips against
Mine

I need
I crave for your body
Against mine
Making sweet beautiful music

I crave
I need

<u>SEPARATION</u>

I am searching
And searching

And yet I cannot find
The answer to this
Broken heart

Could I have seen it
Coming?

The empty promises
The untouched dinners
The unanswered calls
The two beds

My searching is over
The verdict is in
Considering separation
Reconsidering pain

TAKE TIME

Why do you avoid me?
I am trying to hold back
My feelings
But I can't

It's written all over my face
Do you blame me?

Do you wish it went on sed?
I can understand
Why do you treat me this way?

I love you
I really do

Give us a chance
This is not a game
Take time
To reconsider

I need you
I love you

I never meant for it
To be this way

Take time to
See that my feelings
Are real

<u>LOVERS IN THE NIGHT</u>

They both lay there
Contemplating whether to stay or go
For they both share love
In another place
They hold each other tight
Hoping this won't be their
Last night

What if those they love
Never existed?
They fantasize
They hug & kiss
And gaze into
Each other eyes
Without a word they part
Till next time

They are lovers in the night

SHE SAYS

She says she loves you
Yet you are in pain
She says she will never
Walk out on you
Yet you are now a foreigner
In your own state of mind
She says she will not deceive
Nor confuse you
Yet you are starting all over
Trying to put a puzzle together
That you do not understand
She made you a promise
So she says
She promised she will see you
Again
You on the other hand believed
Every word she says

<u>WRONG IN THEIR EYES</u>
<u>RIGHT IN OUR HEARTS</u>

So they see it as something
That is not possible
They question and want
To know what we are
All about
We laugh it off
And gaze into each others eyes
Because only we know
What we have shared
Our hearts communicate in their own
Language
Only you and I understand
That language
They try and try
To figure this love out
But our hearts continue
To flourish we are wrong
So they say
But only you and I
Know what we share
And what we have
Is right in our hearts

TO KNOW

To know you is
To love you
To know that without
You life will never be
The same
For knowing you
I know no pain
To know you is to
Know happiness
Love
&
joy
for no one else can create
the love you possess and share

to know you
to know us

MY BABY

You are finally here
I promise you
I will be there when you cry
I will be your doctor on call
24hrs a day
I will be your chef preparing
All your favorite meals
I will be your counselor
Listening and giving
You advice

I will be your teacher
I will be your leader
Leading you down the right path
I will be your blanket
Warming you up
When ever you are cold
I will be your pillow
Caressing your little head
I will be your shield
Protecting you from evil

My baby most of
All I will be your mother
And your number one friend

A SPECIAL FRIEND

Someone who knows
All about you and
Does not judge you

Someone who accepts you
And understands you
One that will be there
For you
Lending you an ear
Opens up her heart
And reassures you
That everything is going to be
Alright

A special friend
Is always close to your heart

A HEART OF GOLD

Beauty within
The most precious
Gift received
A cherished possession
A miracle
A blessing

A heart of gold

LETTER TO THE WORLD

New days
New age
Have arrived
Freedom has taken
A face lift
Hug yourself
You are alive
You are here
Those around you
Appreciate you
&
love you
life
has a new meaning

live
love
enjoy

for this is a new age
freedom
peace
&
love
are embracing you today

<u>THE LIGHTS OF 9/11</u>

*There they are facing
The sky bright & beautiful*

*It's almost like you can see
The thousandths of souls
Lighting up
Reaching for the sky*

*Some look at the lights
And see
beautiful bright lights
Others see pain, suffering
And anger as well as confusion*

*All those innocent souls
Lost
The lights of 9/11*

*So beautiful so bright
Souls reaching for the sky*

ETERNAL FLAME

Illuminated
Shinning bright for life

Eternal flame
For those who
Cannot be here today
Shinning upon their name
Their memories
Re-living a day
Fill with memories
And pain

Eternal flame
Shinning bright
For eternity

I BELIEVE IN YOU

I believe in you
Do you believe in me?

I know you are all
I need
All I desire
All I ever wanted
I believe in your strength
Your sympathy
And all your desires

I believe you are strong
You are courageous
You will take me till
The end of time

I believe in you
Do you believe in me?

9/10-9/11

As the day approaches
One can help but to wonder
Is it going to happen again?
Are we going to experience
The same fear & pain

How can one treat such a
Fragile day 9/11

A day that made history
A day that changed every ones life
9/11 the day the nation woke up
to realize that it was not a dream
the day our freedom was taken away
the beginning of a long fearful journey
the day that many thought they were just
going to work
the day husbands & wife's
grandparents
&
children
&
friends
gave their love ones
the last kiss of life

the day the nation became one
the heroes became known
9/11
a day that will never be forgotten

NO LONGER PROPERTY

I am free to go
&
explore
'cause I am no longer
your property

I demand my freedom
My sanity
My heart
Consider yourself vacant

Your time is up
I did my bid
I wish to go free now
Hand me the key

I am no longer your property

<u>WHEN WE AGREED</u>

When we agreed to come together
As one I never agreed on pain
When we agreed to love one
Another I meant you and I
When we agreed to stick together
I meant through thick and thin

When we agreed to love
Honor & respect one another
I meant it
We both made an agreement
We both stood there and made
A promise

Do you remember?

When we agreed

I CAN'T EXPLAIN

The words can never explain
The love I thrive
Inside my heart

Forever & ever
Nor
Laughter Nor joy
Could mimic
The strength
The love
I carry within my heart
The dynamics of this love
Will be passed
On without an explanation

IT'S GOING TO BE OK

I understand your pain
Look at me it's going to be ok

Dry you eyes
Lift your spirits
Your heart will mend
Your wounds will heal

Understand your battles
Understand your pain
Dig deep in your soul

Is this the last love
You will ever know?

<u>WHEN I THINK OF YOU</u>

When I think of you
I think of mountains
Bright skies

When I think of you
I think of a miracle
Being brought into the world

When I think of you
I think of all the joy
And happiness you bring
Into my life

I thank the lord for
Making you part
Of my life
My flesh & blood

When I think of you
I think of all the
Wonderful things the
World has to offer

<u>DON'T EVER CALL ME AGAIN</u>

You divulge those powerful
Words to me
'don't ever call me again'
do you really mean them this time?

I have heard those words
So many times before
Then we find ourselves
In contact again

Why is it so hard for us
To remain apart from
One another
We say it's not love
It's just lust
Is it really lust?
Or there is something else there
Do we really care for one another
Deep down inside
Although we are faced with
Obstacles, age difference
&
different morals

once we are in each others
arms nothing really matters
why is that?

Why is it that we cannot be together
Why is it that we are unable
To build unity
We say we love each other
Yet we cannot make time
For one another
So you say
Don't ever call me again

I cannot comprehend that
I will not comprehend
I love you and I know
You love me
Our feelings are more
Than just lust
I leave you with these words

I love you
And I know we will talk again
Till then
Always remember that we
Have more than what we
Bargained for

BEFORE WE PART

Before we part

I must leave you with these words
We have reached a stage where I feel
We served our purpose
We contemplated
And we tried
We gave it our all

Now it's time to part
I must say before you go
That although we are
Moving on
Our hearts will always
Share an abundance of memories

My words are here
To lead you into
This essence of no
Return

A MEMORABLE AFFAIR

A fantasy come true
Wild thunder on a
Summer night
A burning fire
Lingering desire

A powerful voice with
No limitation

A beating heart
Out of restrain

Sweet smelling
Never ending
A new meaning to
The deepest height

THE LETTER

It sat there untouched
On the night table
As I sat there on the chair
Fear and hurt
As well as happiness
Took over my body

This is how it went
To my sweetheart;

I am sorry for all the pain I caused
You don't be shocked by my words
For my words have created pain
I never meant to walk out on you
I just cannot handle the pressure
Your emotions and needs confuse
Me I suffered needless nights
I love us
I love you
Therefore I am departing
Don't be angry
Please forgive me

A SECOND CHANCE

Do second chances
Exist in life?
Are we all entitled to a second
Chance?

Some say yes
Others say they never been fortunate
To experience a second chance

How many second chances
Have you gotten in life?

Consider yourself lucky if
You been given a second chance

<u>GONE</u>

As I sit here and watch you
Lay there with your eyes close
My body begins to tremble

I have been hit with reality
You are now gone
I will no longer hear your voice
Feel your touch
Caress your chest
Kiss your lips

You are gone

I miss you already

A SECOND TIME AROUND

Here we are about to take
A big leap for the
Second time around

Do you promise this time
Is going to be significant
What are you & me going
To do different this
Second time around

Love & trust one another
Or
Hate & hurt each other

Care & nurture one another
Or
Deceive & betray each other

A second time around

<u>MAKING UP YOUR MIND</u>

Hey you calls out that
Inner voice
Come here
"yeah you"
oh, don't act like you
don't hear me
that's what your inner
voice is saying to you
you on the other hand
are moving towards another direction

why is that?
Is it because that inner voice
Controls you
Knows what's right for you
Knows you better than you
Know yourself

"trust me"
says that inner voice
"trust me"

you on the other hand
hope that you are right
for not

listening to that voice
but in reality you are
dead wrong

UNCONDITIONAL LOVE

Why is it so hard to accept it

Some say I love you unconditionally
Are they speaking the truth?
If they are
Why is it that we tend to find ourselves
Judging others by their negative qualities

Unconditional love
In relationships two mates come together
And down the road
Grow apart

If they love each other
Unconditionally why do they remain apart?

Unconditional love
Do you believe that it exist?

ARE WE REALLY FRIENDS

Do real friends betray one another
Do they hurt one another

Are we really friends?

Friends don't lie
To each other

Friends don't turn their back on
One another

Real friends don't allow
Outside influences to
Invade their loyalty

Are we really friends?

I ask you this my friend
Because I now remember
The pain you have caused me

WHEN A HEART ACHES

When a heart aches
It bleeds

When a heart aches
It screams

When a heart aches
It frazzles up the soul

PASSING TIME

Years & years
Have passed
Relationships
&
friendships
have developed
friends have come
and go
lovers made
their contributions

lessons have been taught
rules have been broken
promises have transgressed
secrets have been chosen

A LOST SOUL

As she sat there crying
Calling out for help

No one listen
No one cared

She screamed no one heard her
She begged no one gave her

Vein by vein
Blood began to pour
She continued crying & begging
The lord to forgive her

But the lord was not able to touch her
For her it was to late
She was already lost

Her soul already had an owner

<u>BEHIND THE LOCKED DOOR</u>

The memories are far too many
For he left them embedded in
My memory forever

No one knew him the way
I did
Non stop game playing
Fist burning
Anger brawling

No one saw what I experienced
Up close & personal

Lip bleeding
Hair pulling
Abuse at it's best

For everyone thought
What a beautiful couple

No one saw what went
On behind the locked door

I AM BACK

A weird phone call
In the middle of the night

Awaken
By a strange voice

Strange but yet comforting
The voice went on & on
Without a pause

Tears were streaming
Down my face
The strangers voice began to sound
Very familiar
As I brought the phone closer
To my ears my face lit up
The tears dried up
It was you
Finally I recognized the voice
10 years had passed
10 years!
Dad I shouted and he shouted back
Sorry honey
Please forgive me
Understand that I am back

<u>SEIZE</u>

I seize the pain
I have endured

I seize the love
I have conquered

I seize the road
I have traveled

I seize the moment
We united
And our heart
&
soul
became one

<u>REFLECTIONS</u>

When I look in the mirror
I see someone else

I see a women with fear
&
hidden secrets
&
buried emotions
a lost child that never
made it home
a painful struggle that won't
go away
the complexion is clear
the eyes dark and intense
the stories are untold
the drama unrevealed
I see a stranger
Living the life of someone else
Hiding her true identity
Scared to show the outside
World what she is composed
Of who she really is
What she really thinks

When I look in the mirror
I see a reflection of myself

<u>CAN WE</u>

Can we lay here
An embrace this moment
Like is our last
Breath of air

Can we lay here
And make love
Like is our last day
On earth

Can we caress
Each other
Like is our first time
Together

Can we kiss
One another
And embrace
Each other

Can we

<u>WONDER</u>

Do you ever wonder
What it will be like
If the world had no
Foreign enemies

If we can go back
To 9/11/01
And turn the event into
A fiction movie
Rather than the actual event

If we can accomplish
Peace worldwide
If our leaders can come
Together and resolve
The issues at hand
Without any casualties
Ever wonder

UNTITLED

I will never allow you
Back in my heart

I will never share breathing
Space with you ever
Your evil smile
Plays time and time
Again in my head
The thought of you
Pounding on my delicate skin
Pulling on the strands
You once loved to
Twirl your fingers through
Slapping the face you once
Caress
Bruising the heart you
Once conquered
Busting the lips you
Once kissed
Ripping through with force the canal
That once brought you life

I am walking away
Forgetting all the pain
You brought yesterday

<u>WITH THIS RING</u>

With this ring you profess
Will you be mine forever

With this ring you say
Let's pretend
Everything from the past
Will vanish

With this ring you want
To erase deep scars
That are forever embedded
You want to buy lost love

You want to pretend
&
forget

with the ring on
one hand
my bleeding broken
heart in the other
I must say
Sorry my emotions
My life

My heart
Are not for sale

So with this ring
I must say no I can
I will never

FAILED RELATIONSHIPS

We once were an item
Holding hands making love
Swearing nothing will tear
Us apart

Staying up all hours of the night
Hugging & kissing
Caressing one another
Enjoying every single moment

Now we do nothing
But swear at each other
In negative ways

We don't make love anymore
We act as if we are strangers

Where did we go wrong?
I guess this is it
You go your way and
I'll go mine
Always remember we once were
In love
And now we are strangers

Good bye my love
Good bye my x- lover
Good luck in your next journey

TILL DEATH DO US PART

So you have given
Me all you have
Wow, it's that it?

You always claim you will never
Give up and now I am learning
That you have lied

It's not that easy to get out
We have a contract together
Do you remember

'till death do us part'

you gave me your word
and I gave you mine
and now you want to give up
sorry, but I am not going to
let you go
tell that cloud it's
got a fight on it's hands
tell" it" you are not alone
you made me a promise
come on
go ahead

face me
your eyes where always so bright
today they seem tired
are you really giving up on me?
Are you brave enough to leave me?
Well guess what "it" does not stand
A chance
Yeah I know it makes you feel
Like you are on cloud nine
But I am sure I make you feel better

Baby I am less expensive
I am attainable
I am your rock
Please come back
You have not given me all
You've got
It's ok the feeling will pass
I will stand by you
Please honey
'till death do us part'
remember that
I leave you now with
These few words
I can forgive you
The material stuff is replaceable
You are not
I forgive you
It does not
It will take you to your grave
Determinate all we've got

Please
Come back
I see your eyes moving your
Body shivering
It's finally going away
Is that worth us?
A 20 minute high
A 5 minute ride

Please honey
Don't allow it
To take you
To the other side
Please honey

'till death do us part'

<u>TELL ME WHAT YOU SEE</u>

Tell me what you see

I see a women of courage
A precious stone
A priceless diamond

A heart of gold
I see struggle
I see pain
I see lonely roads
I see rivers overflowing

A lonely child
Waiting to be held
I see a rainbow

I no longer see darkness
I now see the light

Tell me what you see
Tell me what's ahead

Answer me please

IT'S OVER NOW

Why can you understand
That is over now
All the pain & suffering
Is ending now
How many scars can I trace
Back to you
Where did it go
Let me tell you
You decided to mistreat me
You decided to mislead me
Yeah you
You made decisions for me
Yeah you
All the pain and tears have
Finally dried up
All the memories are fading away
Thank you for the deep scars you
Have tattooed on my heart
They are not visible by the naked eye
But they are there buried and hidden
Where my soul lies
Please understand that I no longer
Wish to see you
Nor hear your voice
Or let along feel your touch

Finally I have the courage to walk
Away and say goodbye

<u>FEAR</u>

What is fear?
The feeling of rejection
Staring at you in the face
When you are attempting
To move forward

Fear
The inner voice you hear
When something is not right
The feeling of a wall crumbling
Down on you
The dark room that won't
Light up
The door that won't open up
The dark shadow that walks
Beside you

Fear

RELATIONSHIPS

Love
Hate
Lust
Honesty and trust

What makes a relationship?
An honest companion
A loving person

Someone who looks for someone
Else to share a part of them
Someone who feels that is time
To come together and be one

What is a relationship?

Your last phone call when you
Go to bed at night
Your heart saying I do

A relationship is what you
Make of it
A relationship is based on
Trust & understanding

A CREATION OF YOUR PRESENCE

Your eyes caught me by surprise
Your smile made me realize
That you too were thinking
About me

Your flirtatious ways
Your lovable & huggable body
Your beautiful lips
Made me crave

You and only you
Can explain this abundance
Of joy & happiness

For it all belongs
To you

A creation of your presence

A STRANGERS SMILE

I looked at you
You looked back at me
We both smiled
At one another
From across the crowd
But unfortunately I lost you

Wow I thought to myself
Where did he go
Why did I not reach out

As I walked down the street
I spotted you once again
But all I was able to say
Was hello

And once again
We both smile

<u>PHYSICALLY NOT</u>
<u>EMOTIONALLY</u>

The time has now come
I don't know where to start

I have to tell you that I
Never thought we will
See this day
It's tough to think you
Are going away
This is not what we expected
Let's not frown
We have shared good times
And we most move on
Our hearts and soul
are made for one another
Let's not forget that
We love each other
That's what matters
Separation is what is requested
Physically but emotionally
And mentally
Parting ways does not
Exist in our hearts

ABOUT THE AUTHOR

She was born in the Bronx, the youngest daughter of two Dominican immigrants that immigrated to the United States in search of the American dream. Following her college graduation in 1999 from John Jay college of Criminal Justice in New York City, Isabel then went on to become one of New York's finest by joining the Police Department in 2000.

The best choice that was made in her behalf by her family was ensuring she received an education. Growing up in an era where dropping out of school was the "in" thing to do, her parents became dictators. Her dad will constantly say to her "mijita la escuela es muy importante, no te lleves de tus amigas". Translation; daughter of mine school is very important don't allow your friends to influence you. She never judge herself to be an excellent student. She developed an abhorrence towards all her subjects. Proven critical as she later struggled to make it out of college. She sought writing as a form of therapy; she kept numerous journals throughout her journey. She now finds herself in a new era, furthering her writing has become her number one priority. She has currently enrolled in City College and is working towards her masters in creative writing.

This is just the beginning for this new up and coming author, look out for her next big project.